CONTENTS

Book published in association with
www.rockettplumbing.co.uk

DAILY ECHO

CHAMPION

CHERRIES CLINCH LEAGUE TITLE... P2,3,4,5

FOREWORD

WHILE recent events may have somewhat eclipsed this club's previous history, it is important not to forget the past.

Promotion to the Premier League is a reward for everybody associated with AFC Bournemouth and will hopefully herald the dawn of another exciting era.

This book, a pictorial trip down memory lane, references most of the highs and lows since the club was founded in 1899 and contains some fantastic photographs.

I have been honoured and privileged to have watched, played for and managed this great club and have made no secret of the fact I hold it very close to my heart.

I first started watching the team after I had moved here in the 1980s and count myself fortunate to have seen Harry Redknapp's great team win promotion to the second tier in 1987.

It was a squad packed with excellent players and took the club into uncharted territory following years spent in the bottom two divisions after joining the Football League in 1923.

Another of the club's momentous seasons came in 1956-57 when Freddie Cox and his players beat Wolves and Tottenham before losing to Manchester United in the quarter-final of the FA Cup.

Having worked closely with Kevin Bond when he was manager here, I know how proud he was of his father's achievements at Dean Court in the early 1970s.

I was lucky to spend time in the company of John Bond, a very knowledgeable football man and a real gentleman, and the days of Ted MacDougall and co are rightly legendary among supporters.

During my apprenticeship, I watched Mel Machin mastermind the Great Escape before experiencing first-hand the administration of 1997.

Although they were both tough times for very different reasons, the spirit and resolve among players and supporters really came to the fore and demonstrated how much the club means to so many people.

Honoured to represent the club at Wembley in 1998, I was present at the Millennium Stadium to witness another tumultuous day when Sean O'Driscoll's team won the Division Three play-off final in 2003.

The administration of 2008 was another testing time but, thanks largely to the efforts of our current chairman Jeff Mostyn, the club pulled through and lived to fight another day.

It has certainly been an eventful journey and one which this book depicts perfectly.

Up the Cherries!

Eddie Howe

Eddie Howe - AFC Bournemouth Manager

Book published in association with
www.rockettplumbing.co.uk

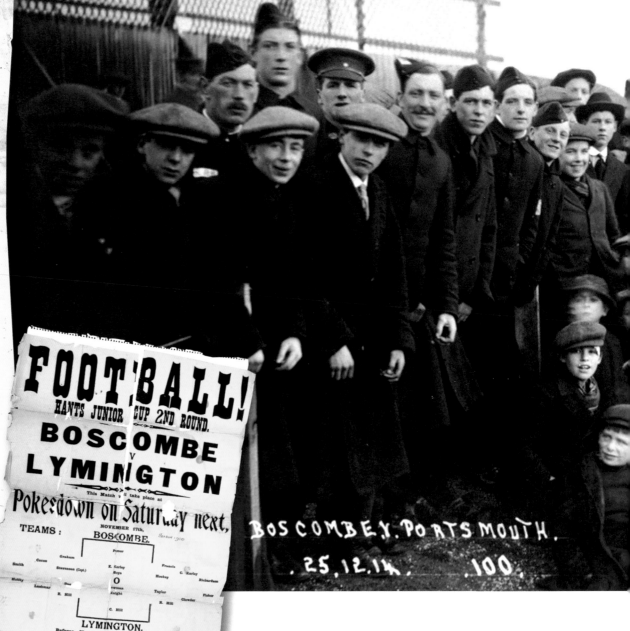

FOOTBALL! FOOTBALL

BOURNEMOUTH & DISTRICT
JUNIOR FOOTBALL LEAGUE,
SEASON 1898-99.

AN
INTER-LEAGUE MATCH
WILL BE PLAYED ON
WEDNESDAY, APRIL 26, 1899,
ON THE
POKESDOWN FOOTBALL GROUND
CASTLEMAINE ROAD, POKESDOWN.
DRESSING ROOM: "THE PINE CLIFF HOTEL"

The President of the League, J. A. NETHERCOATE, ESQ., will kick off at 5 p.m.

The following Players will represent the HANTS. and DORSET SECTIONS of the League:

DORSET:

WILKINS (Vice-Capt.) 'Hamworthy St. Michael's'
BLANDFORD 'Arabs'

A. GALTON 'Parkstone'
WILKINS 'Hamworthy'

HANDS 'Arabs'
BAILEY 'Parkstone'

ADLEM 'Longfleet S. Mary's'
T. BROWN 'Hamworthy S. Michael's'

PAUL 'Arabs'
ANDREWS 'Longfleet St. Mary's'

DUNFORD (Capt.) 'Parkstone'
WEEKS 'Longfleet St. Mary's'

JEFFREY 'Arabs'
N. EDWARDS 'Longfleet S. Mary's'

NEWMAN 'Longfleet St. Mary's'
W. DUNFORD 'Parkstone'

MOORE 'Longfleet S. Mary's'
S. GALTON 'Parkstone'

S. BROWN 'Longfleet St. Mary's'
REAL 'Arabs'

COURT 'Hamworthy S. Michael's'
SLATTERY 'Parkstone'

BOYS 'Pokesdown'

MARSH 'Pokesdown'
ANSLOW 'Reserves'

BELLOWS 'Pokesdown'
HAYES 'United'

BROOK 'Rovers'
GIBBONS 'Reserves'

MILLER 'United'
W. GRAHAM 'Reserves'

Dorset play in their respective Club colours.

SHUTLER and J. HAXELL.

LADIES FREE.

WALTER J. TAYLOR, Hon. Sec.

TEAM CARD
PRICE ONE PENNY
Bristol City v. Boscombe
Dean Court, Boscombe   Saturday, 22nd September 1945

BOSCOMBE
BIRD
Goal

MARSDEN
2—Right Full Back
SIMPSON
3—Left Full Back

BUSBY
WILSON
3—Centre Half Back
SUMMERBEE
6—Left Half Back

L. C. FINCH
PATON
THOMAS
9—Centre Forward
FIELDING
10—Inside Left
McDONALD
11—Outside Left

SHILCOTT
WILLIAMS
CLARK
9—Centre Forward
CURRAN
8—Inside Right
COLLINS
7—Outside Right

PREECE
ROBERTS
Centre Half Back
MORGAN
4—Right Half Back

BAILEY
3—Left Full Back
GUY
2—Right Full Back

SILCOCKS
Goal

BRISTOL CITY.
Kick-off 3 p.m.

Football League. Div. 3. Southern Section.

SCORE. Boscombe 8   Bristol C. 1

FOOTBALL!
HANTS JUNIOR CUP 2ND ROUND.
BOSCOMBE
v
LYMINGTON
This Match will take place at
Pokesdown on Saturday next,
NOVEMBER 17th,

TEAMS:
BOSCOMBE.

LYMINGTON.
Referee, Mr J. C. Le Grand, Southampton.

Kick-Off 2.15. Admission 3d. All Pay.

J. E. TREW, Printer, Boscombe.

BOSCOMBE V. PORTSMOUTH.
25.12.14.   100.

THE EARLY YEARS
1890-1949

AFC Bournemouth began life as Boscombe St John's Lads Institute FC in 1890.

But the Cherries story really began on October 7, 1899, when Boscombe FC played its first match. The venue was a pitch in Castlemain Road, the opponents were Christchurch Royal Artillery, and the visitors won 2-1.

Kings Park became the Cherries' home in 1902, and in 1910, landowner JE Cooper-Dean granted a long lease on a piece of waste ground there. Club secretary Wilf Hayward enlisted volunteers to build a stand for 300 spectators.

The club lifted the Hampshire Junior Cup in 1905-06 and made their FA Cup debut in 1913-14 but were struggling in the South-Eastern League when war cut the season short.

After the war, the club won at least one trophy a season until 1923, when they became Bournemouth and Boscombe Athletic FC and entered the Football League.

The remaining inter-war years were a period of highs and lows. The lows included twice dropping out of the League; their worst-ever season in 1933-34, with 100 goals conceded; and the first time the Cherries had to get out the begging bowl.

The highs included reaching the third round of the FA Cup in 1926-27, with 13,409 watching them at home against Liverpool; gaining a new stand for 3,700 spectators; and beating Northampton 10-0 at Dean Court, only for the outbreak of World War II the next day to wipe the result from the record books.

In 1946, the Cherries won their first major trophy, the League Three (South) Cup, after a 136-minute semi-final replay against QPR at Shepherds Bush.

That April, a promotion battle with QPR saw 25,700 in the ground at Dean Court and 6,000 outside listening to a commentary by the secretary. It was QPR who went up that season, but a proud Boscombe set nine club records.

- LEFT: Boscombe FC 1899-1900 season - the first Cherries team photo
- TOP RIGHT: 1906-07
- MIDDLE RIGHT: 1908-09
- BOTTOM RIGHT: 1910-11

1899-1911   Cherries played at Castlemain Road, Pokesdown from 1899-1902 then at Kings Park from 1910

BOSCOMBE WINNERS OF WEST HANTS AND PAGE CROFT CUPS · 1912-13 PHOTO BY Co .244.

Season tickets were first issued in 1912-13, grandstand tickets were 10s.6d. per year and ground season tickets were 5s

1912-1913

13.4.1914. BOSCOMBE V. BOURNEMOUTH. 328.

■ OPPOSITE TOP LEFT: Spectators at Boscombe v Bournemouth 3rd January 1913

■ OPPOSITE TOP RIGHT: Boscombe FC crowd 1920

■ OPPOSITE BOTTOM LEFT: Photo dated 28th April 1920 shows the old main stand.

■ OPPOSITE BOTTOM RIGHT: Boscombe FC winners Page Croft Cup 1920

1913-1920   Crowd in the stands at Boscombe v Bournemouth football match 13th April 1914

BOSCOMBE V. BOURNEMOUTH JAN.3.1913 .168.

With the declaration of war, the South-Eastern League ceased to run and the club no longer played

1913-1920

■ BELOW: Aerial view of Dean Court 1927

■ TOP RIGHT: Boscombe team Southern League 1921

■ BOTTOM RIGHT: Mr CE Sutcliffe (Vice President of the Football League) opens new stand

1921-1927

In 1923 the club changed its name to Bournemouth and Boscombe Athletic

- BELOW: 1926-27
- TOP RIGHT: 1926-27
- TOP CENTRE: Cartoon from The Football Echo and Sports Gazette Saturday August 8th 1926
- BOTTOM MIDDLE: 1931-32
- BOTTOM RIGHT: 1932-33

The club was managed from 1923-25 by Harry Kinghorn and from 1925-28 by Leslie Knighton

1926-1933

A GOALKEEPER'S VIEW OF **SURTEES** AT INSIDE-RIGHT FOR BOSCOMBE

AN OPPOSING FORWARD'S **VIEW OF C.H.WILSON** AT RIGHT-BACK

AND A WHOLE FORWARD LINE'S **VIEW OF COEN** IN GOAL.

OTHER PEOPLE'S POINTS OF VIEW

1932-1933

Cartoon from The Football Echo and Sports Gazette October 8th 1933

- ABOVE: Boscombe football team and directors annual outing 1935
- BELOW: Team 1936-37
- TOP RIGHT: Team 1937-38

- BOTTOM RIGHT: Boscombe team group, 1937-38. Back row left to right: Willie Smith, Norman Millar, Len Brooks, Fred Pincott, Fred Marsden, Peter Monaghan. Front row left to right: Bob Redfern, Ernie Whittam, Harry Mardon, Willie O'Brien, Jimmy Lovery

Bob Crompton managed the team from 1935-36 and Charlie Bell from 1936-39

1936-1938

1937-1938

1937 Aerial shot of Dean Court, Thistlebarrow Road

Back row left to right: Dai Woodward, Fred Rowell, Fred Wilson, Ken Bird, Joe Sanaghan, Paddy Gallacher. Front Row: left to right: Tommy Paton, Jack Kirkham, Fred Marsden, Ernie Tagg, Jack McDonald

The 1945-46 League Division 3 (South) cup winning team

1945-1946

1945-1946   Cherries play Queen's Park Rangers at home in their semi-final tie in the Southern Section Cup after the War

The Dean Courtier: "I shall have to cram this lot into that goal somehow."

A busy month is reflected in a cartoon from The Football Echo and Sports Gazette Saturday September 7th, 1946

1946-1947

17

■ BELOW: Boscombe overcome a
two goal half-time deficit to win
their FA Cup tie 4-1 against Exeter
City to inspire this cartoon in the
Football Echo and Sports Gazette
Saturday December 7th 1946

DEEP
DEPRESSION

HA! HA!
I'M FROM
EXETER

I WISH I
HAD NEVER
LEFT THE
SEA

Half-time:-
BOSCOMBE .. 0
EXETER CITY .. 2

Full-time:-
BOSCOMBE .. 4
EXETER CITY .. 2

1946-1948

Match against Wolverhampton Wanderers attracts largest FA Cup tie crowd at Dean Court

■ BELOW: Bournemouth and Boscombe Athletic team photo 1947-48 season

RIGHT: Boscombe players Percival, Bennett and Bird training at YMCA for cup tie with Manchester United January 1949

1947-1949

1948-1949

Boscombe players in Manchester for cup tie with Manchester United 10th January 1949

■ FAR LEFT: Boscombe team 1948-49

■ LEFT: Boscombe first team for the Golden Jubilee season 1949-50

FA Cup 3rd round, the Boscombe defence under pressure against Manchester United in front of 55,012 at Maine Road

1948-1949

1948-1949

ABOVE: Jack Percival cartoon from The Football Echo and Sports Gazette Saturday October 8 1948

ABOVE: Ken Bird shakes hands with Notts County's Tommy Lawton on the occasion of his benefit match and 200th match appearance

■ BELOW: Boscombe get some hints from trainer 'Dick' Mellors. Players from left to right: Sinclair, Marsh, Duke, Bartholomew, Drummond, Fisher with Johnston and Buchanan kneeling

1949-1950

Bournemouth & Boscombe
ATHLETIC FOOTBALL CLUB

No 6568

OFFICIAL
SOUVENIR
PROGRAMME

6d

SATURDAY, FEBRUARY 16th, 1957

BOURNEMOUTH AND BOSCOMBE

VERSUS

TOTTENHAM HOTSPUR

F.A. CUP — ROUND 5

KICK - OFF 3 p.m.

WHO'S AFRAID OF THE BIG BAD WOLVES!

Football broadcast for hospitals

THE FIFTIES

It was a match that would be talked about for a lifetime – the day Bournemouth and Boscombe Athletic took on the Busby Babes.

Manchester United came to Dean Court to play before a crowd of 28,799, bringing with them the astonishing crop of young players who had been nurtured by Sir Matt Busby.

Boscombe had already seen an astonishing cup run, beating Burton Albion 8-0, Swindon 1-0, Accrington Stanley 2-0, Wolves 1-0 (a result hailed as the greatest giant-killing in history) and Spurs 3-1.

Boscombe's Brian Bedford scored once, United's Johnny Berry twice. All the goals, especially United's winning penalty, were controversial, but the Cherries had made a great side sweat.

Less than a year after the match, six of that visiting team were killed in the Munich air disaster.

Cherries set a new record that year for the most goals in a season – 88 in the League, 16 in the Cup.

The match was the highlight of a decade which had started with the Cherries' golden jubilee season but had then seen some inconsistent football.

Highlights had included the signing in 1952 of Tommy Goodwin from Leicester. His recall to Eire in 1956 made him the first full international to play for Boscombe.

After the Manchester United clash, the Cherries would see a couple of mediocre seasons, finishing the decade mid-table in the new, national Division Three.

But the memory of United would last a lifetime. Busby wrote in his memoirs: "There were many great Cup occasions for United in 1956/57, yet I feel our finest hour was seen on the Dean Court ground at Bournemouth."

Book published in association with
www.rockettplumbing.co.uk

ROCKETT
PLUMBING & HEATING SUPPLIES LTD

■ John Meadows, Boscombe's goalkeeper, making a double-fisted clearance over the head of Roost, Bristol Rovers' inside-left. Boscombe won 2-0 March 1951

1950-1952

■ BELOW: 17th September 1952, Bournemouth and Boscombe Athletic lose 2-1 against Newport County

ABOVE RIGHT: Tommy Godwin tries an acrobatic save while Jack Fisher watches on, 7th November 1953

1952-1953

■ Boscombe's Godwin dives too late when Day (out of picture) scored the Saints first goal

1953-1954

The Boscombe defence under pressure against Southampton at the Dell, Southampton won 2-1

■ 21st August 1954, Coventry City beat Bournemouth and Boscombe Athletic 1-0

1954-1955

LEFT: Joseph "Joe" Brown played for Boscombe from 1954-59

■ LEFT: Derek Leaver going for goal. 24th August 1955. Bournemouth and Boscombe Athletic beat Colchester United 3-1

■ RIGHT: Charles "Charlie" Gallogly played as a fullback for Huddersfield Town, Watford and Bournemouth. In 1950 he won two caps for Northern Ireland

ABOVE: 9th October 1954, Bournemouth and Boscombe Athletic beaten 1-0 by Millwall

1954-1955

■ LEFT: Reg Hayward, left, welcomes Freddie Cox, right, Boscombe's new manager in April 1956

■ BELOW LEFT: Bournemouth and Boscombe Athletic v Coventry City, team photo 1955-56

■ BELOW RIGHT: Derek Reeves scores for Saints, 1st October 1955. Bournemouth and Boscombe Athletic lose 1-3 against Southampton

1955-1957 RIGHT: Laurie Cunningham attempts to block the shot of Southampton's Derek Reeves, but the ball ends up in the net

Who's afraid of the big, bad Wolves? Not these Cherries fans!

1956-1957

■ LEFT: Cherries supporters during the 1956-57 season FA Cup run

■ BOTTOM LEFT: FA Cup action against Wolverhampton Wanderers

■ RIGHT: Walking off at half-time after the collision between Bill Slater and Hughes, Boscombe centre-half. Hughes is second from right and Slater is being carried off

■ BELOW: Reg Cutler, left, staggers out after breaking the Wolves goalpost. The game was held up for several minutes

1956-1957

Reg Cutler breaks the Wolves goalpost!

■ BELOW: Reg Cutler kisses the boot that put Wolves out of the FA Cup and Boscombe into the fifth round. Others in the dressing room picture, left to right: Nelson Stiffle, Joe Brown, Stan Newsham, Lew Clayton, Oliver Norris and Arnold Woollard

■ TOP RIGHT: The players celebrate

■ BOTTOM RIGHT: It was a great day for Tommy Godwin, Boscombe's goalkeeper hero in the FA Cup-tie with Wolverhampton. His father journeyed from Dublin to see him play

Boscombe win 1-0 to go through to the fifth round of the FA Cup!

1956-1957

- LEFT: Boscombe's no.1 supporter, Sheila Parsons, queues for tickets in the enclosure. Twenty one year old Sheila plans to throw a party for the Boscombe team
- RIGHT: Boscombe goalkeeper Bill Ellaway
- BELOW: Early arrivals at Dean Court at 9 o'clock in the morning

1956-1957

Cherries take on Spurs in the FA Cup 5th round

■ BELOW: Stan Newsham beats the Spurs goalkeeper with a fine header

■ MIDDLE: St. John Ambulance men and police treat injured spectators on the touch line

■ RIGHT: Bournemouth goalkeeper Tommy Godwin had another great match, here he is tipping one round the post

Bournemouth beat Spurs 3-1 to go through to 6th round of the FA Cup!

1956-1957

■ LEFT: Sir Matt Busby on the pitch before the game

■ BOTTOM LEFT: Boscombe and Bournemouth team led off the field by Ollie Norris at half time, 1-0 up against the Man United team

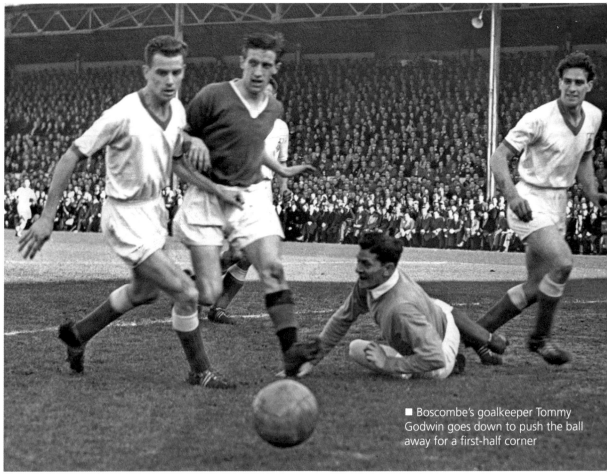

■ Boscombe's goalkeeper Tommy Godwin goes down to push the ball away for a first-half corner

1956-1957

It's the FA Cup 6th round against the mighty Manchester United

■ LEFT: BBC commentators Alan Clark and Raymond Glendenning. Bournemouth & Boscombe Athletic v Manchester United 2nd March 1957, Attendance: 28,799
■ BELOW: Ollie Norris challenges Man United keeper Ray Wood

■ LEFT: Freddie Cox with the team when they were awarded the Sunday Pictorial Giant Killers cup
■ BOTTOM RIGHT: Enthusiastic supporters rush onto the pitch at the end of the match and police form a lane to allow players to leave the field

Bournemouth lose 1-2 and the great FA Cup run is over

1956-1957

■ ABOVE: Bournemouth & Boscombe Athletic 1959-60

1957-1959

ABOVE: Panoramic shot of Dean Court featuring a match against Brentford in October 1959

GREAT NORTHERN VICTORIA HOTEL

Bournemouth & Boscombe Athletic arriving at Bradford in 1960

Match of decade grips Bournemouth

£885,000 grant for B'mouth by-pass

'AIN'T GOT THIS THOUGH,' said the gentleman with the sideboards and the red-and-white scarf

Bournemouth & Boscombe
ATHLETIC FOOTBALL CLUB

BOURNEMOUTH & BOSCOMBE ATHLETIC FOOTBALL CLUB

OFFICIAL PROGRAMME

WEDNESDAY, 20th NOVEMBER, 1968

BOURNEMOUTH & BOSCOMBE

CUP PHOTO-SPECIAL

FOUR MINUTES TO GO...

Liverpool skipper

By COLIN SMITH

IT IS FOUR MINUTES FROM TIME AND BOSCOMBE, A GOAL UP IN THEIR F.A. CUP CLASH AT DEAN COURT, ARE STUNNED BY A DISPUTED LIVERPOOL EQUALISER. IT'S A DRAW, AND A RE-PLAY AT ANFIELD IS REQUIRED.

th JANUARY, 1966

AND BOSCOMBE

RK RANGERS

KICK-OFF 3 p.m.

THE SIXTIES

In the decade when England celebrated its national team's World Cup triumph, the action at Dean Court was often a lot less inspiring.

Starting the decade mid-table in Division Three, Boscombe struggled, and manager Don Welsh was sacked in 1961.

His replacement was the team's first player-manager, Bill McGarry, who had captained Huddersfield and been capped for England four times.

McGarry presided over a recovery, and even a shot at promotion in 1962-63. His successor, Reg Flewin, also led a serious promotion challenge.

Freddie Cox succeeded him for a second stint as manager, but the Cherries were plagued by declining gates (below 4,000 at the end of 1965), cash shortages and disappointing results. They finished 20th in the division in 1966-67.

But there were morale-boosting occasions too. In January 1968, a Dean Court crowd of 24,388 saw the Cherries apply pressure to a Liverpool team that included Emlyn Hughes, Ian Callaghan and Ian St John. The goalless FA Cup third round match led to a replay at Anfield, when Boscombe played strongly but were defeated 4-1.

The same year saw ex-player Dickie Dowsett launch the Cherry Bees fundraising initiative, plus the opening of a supporters club. Kick-offs at 7.30pm on Saturdays until the end of September were designed to draw holiday-makers and those who played other sports on Saturday afternoons.

The team were playing sufficiently well to be promotion hopefuls in 1968-69. That would all go sour the following season, but in the summer of 1969, Cox spent perhaps the best £10,000 the club had ever parted with – buying a young striker named Ted MacDougall.

Book published in association with
www.rockettplumbing.co.uk

■ LEFT: Cllr WJ Wareham, president of Dean Court football supporters club, handing over new metal gates at Dean Court to chairman Reg Hayward, to commemorate the diamond jubilee of the club

■ BELOW: Boscombe Football Club chairman Mr RT Hayward, holding the Pickford Cup, and manager Don Welsh chat to ground staff boys Bob Trote, Chris Reading, Tony Adlen, Tony Byrne and Ray Massey at the Bournemouth Pavilion Feb 1960

■ TOP RIGHT: Aerial view of Boscombe including AFC Bournemouth and Boscombe railway line, taken in 1960

■ BOTTOM RIGHT: Match action from April 1961

1960-1961

Cherries celebrate their diamond jubilee with new gates at Dean Court

RIGHT: Boscombe and Bournemouth Athletic team from 4th November 1961

BOTTOM RIGHT: Match action from 16th September 1961

LEFT: Construction of Dean Court tower bases for the new floodlights in June 1961

1961-1962

■ RIGHT: St John Ambulance girls waiting for the players to go on the pitch, September 1961

■ BELOW RIGHT: Bill McGarry signs for Bournemouth as the club's player-manager in March 1961

1961-1962

LEFT: Floodlit Dean Court from September 1961

■ LEFT: Action from September 1962

■ BELOW: Goalkeeper David Best

RIGHT: Snow covers Dean Court in January 1963 but training continues

1962-1963

■ TOP LEFT: Team photo for 1962-63 season

■ TOP RIGHT: Action from the 1962-63 season

■ BOTTOM RIGHT: Team photo for 1963-64 season

1962-1964   BOTTOM LEFT: Denis Coughlin misses a penalty as Bournemouth draw 1-1 with Walsall in April 1964

LEFT: New trainer John Kirk

RIGHT: Bournemouth and Boscombe Athletic Football Club photo call from pre-season 1965

ABOVE LEFT: The new stand being erected at Dean Court in August 1964

1964-1966

■ LEFT: New floodlights being used by Cherries fans to get a better view

■ CENTRE: Bournemouth and Boscombe team 22nd October 1965

■ BELOW CENTRE: Keeper David Best in FA Cup action against Weymouth on 13th November 1965. They drew 0-0, but won the replay in Weymouth 1-4

■ Bournemouth manager Freddie Cox contemplates how his team can beat Burnley FC in the FA Cup 3rd round at Dean Court. The match ended in a 1-1 draw

1965-1966

In early 1966 Bournemouth draw Burnley in the FA Cup 3rd round

■ ABOVE: Home fans cheer on as Boscombe draw the FA Cup match against Burnley 1-1

■ BELOW: Tony Hancock in the crowd at Dean Court for the FA Cup match against Burnley

■ MIDDLE AND BELOW: The Bournemouth team and enthusiastic fans travel a full 24 hours by train to see the FA Cup 3rd round replay against Burnley

■ BOTTOM LEFT: Bournemouth lose the match 7-0, Andy Lochhead (on knees), Dave Merrington (arms raised), and goalie Dave Best

Bournemouth earn a 1-1 draw at home, but in the replay fans see their team beaten 7-0 at Burnley

1965-1966

■ Action from a home defeat by Scunthorpe United

Cherries played Watford twice in League Division Three in April 1966. Cherries won 2-0 at home and lost 1-0 away

1965-1966

1965-1966

Bournemouth and Boscombe Athletic v Torquay United, 1st October 1966. Bournemouth won 1-0

1966-1967

■ Roger Jones, goalkeeper in action at Dean Court in 1966

■ BELOW: New signing Phil Ferns (Senior) with manager Reg Flewin

■ RIGHT: Supporters from Portchester School cheer on Boscombe FC against Walthamstow

■ BOTTOM CENTRE AND RIGHT: Fans queue for admission to Cherries' match against Bury and the chance to buy tickets for the FA Cup tie against Liverpool. First in the queue were Mr and Mrs Bill Durham who arrived at 8.15am

1966-1968   Fans queue in the rain for the chance to buy tickets for the third round FA Cup tie against Liverpool January 1968

■ RIGHT: A section of the near 25,00 crowd at Dean Court for the FA Cup 3rd round tie against Liverpool on 27th January 1968

■ FAR RIGHT: The Liverpool team arrive at Hurn Airport in January 1968 for their FA Cup 3rd round tie against Bournemouth. Ian St John is seen at the front with bag and Emlyn Hughes is fourth from left facing away from camera

■ BELOW LEFT: FA Cup action against Liverpool. The match ended in a 0-0 draw

■ BOTTOM RIGHT: Tony Hately heads Liverpool's first goal in their 4-1 victory over Bournemouth in the replay at Anfield on 30th January 1968

Bournemouth and Boscombe Athletic v Liverpool, FA Cup 3rd round January 1968

1967-1968

■ LEFT: Happy young supporters at Dean Court among a near 10,000 gate for the FA Cup tie against Bury. Cherries won 3-0

■ BELOW: Playing staff for the 1968-69 season

■ RIGHT: Ted MacDougall moved from York City in July 1969 for a fee of £10,000

■ BOTTOM RIGHT: Young fans at Dean Court in April 1969

1968-1969

Ted MacDougall signs for Bournemouth from York City

- BELOW AND BOTTOM LEFT: John Hold in action in September 1969
- BOTTOM CENTRE: Action from 1st November 1969
- RIGHT: There was no denying these youngsters as they invaded the Dean Court pitch at the final whistle to pay tribute to their heroes who had beaten First Division Sheffield Wednesday 1-0 in the FA Cup
- BOTTOM RIGHT: Tony Powell in action at Dean Court in March 1970

LEFT AND ABOVE LEFT: Bournemouth's John Hold in action in September 1969

1969-1970

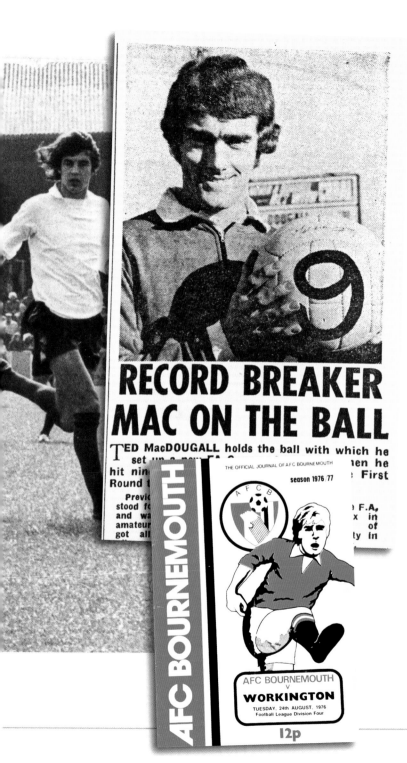

THE SEVENTIES

It was the decade of Supermac.

The Cherries started the 1970s by being relegated to the Fourth Division, but bounced straight back up with the aid of one of the club's legends.

MacDougall set a club record of 49 goals in that season of 1970-71, including six against Oxford City in the FA Cup.

Manager John Bond strengthened the squad with further signings, including Phil Boyer, with whom MacDougall continued the phenomenal partnership which had begun at York.

Bond also introduced the name AFC Bournemouth and adopted red and black shirts inspired by AC Milan.

The Cherries were on top form again for most of 1971-72, with MacDougall scoring nine goals in the 11-0 demolition of Margate in the FA Cup. But their form slipped later on and they missed out on promotion.

Bond made two more key signings: Jimmy Gabriel from Southampton and Harry Redknapp from West Ham. But in September 1972, MacDougall was bought by Manchester United for £200,000. For the second time in a row, the Cherries narrowly missed out on promotion.

John Bond was lured to Norwich in 1973, along with coach Ken Brown, followed by a succession of key players.

One of those, John Benson, returned to Dean Court as player-manager in 1978, by which time the club was troublingly close to dropping out of the Fourth Division.

MacDougall was also back in November 1978, but too many games were going the wrong way, and Benson quit.

New manager Alec Stock presided over a morale-boosting 7-1 win against Doncaster – but few could have predicted the success that would follow in just a few years.

Book published in association with
www.rockettplumbing.co.uk

ROCKETT
PLUMBING & HEATING SUPPLIES LTD

■ LEFT: Dennis Allen in action during Bournemouth v Workington 23rd September 1970, they won 1-0, League Division 4

■ BOTTOM LEFT: Training in the snow on the Fernheath Road ground. Led by Keith Miller, Trevor Hartley and John Sainty

■ RIGHT: West Ham's Billy Bonds and Bournemouth's David Stocks await the fall of the coin in a pre-season practice game

1970-1971   ABOVE RIGHT: Phil Boyer and Ted MacDougall in sombrero hats looking forward to the 1970 World Cup in Mexico

- LEFT: Bournemouth team 1st May 1971
- BOTTOM CENTRE: Alan Sharp of the Coverdale Organisation discusses 'positive play as a result of positive thinking' training scheme with John Bond, Ken Brown, Harold Walker and Reg Tyrell
- BOTTOM RIGHT: Harold Walker and Ken Brown share a joke with the team after 8-1 win at Dean Court in the FA Cup replay against City in November 1970

- BELOW: Manager John Bond with new signing goalkeeper Fred Davies

TOP RIGHT: John Bond in talks with West Ham's Harry Redknapp in December 1970. He transferred two years later for £31,000

1970-1971

■ TOP LEFT: Dean Court pitch is ploughed up for levelling and improved drainage May 1971

■ ABOVE CENTRE AND RIGHT: Hush-hush practice match against Arsenal at the Bournemouth Water Company ground

■ BOTTOM LEFT: Scoreboard from Bournemouth v Cardiff advertising the Southampton match pictured right

■ BOTTOM CENTRE: Friendly against Southampton at Dean Court. Boscombe skipper Keith Miller clashes with Southampton full back Denis Hollywood who was booked and also conceded a penalty. Bournemouth won 3-2 4th August 1971

1971-1972   TOP RIGHT CENTRE: Arsenal captain Frank McLintock leads his team out for a secret match in August 1971

Cherries fly to Guernsey for a four-day stay at the Vale Recreation Club on the island August 1971

1971-1972

■ ABOVE RIGHT: John Bond and 14 year old son Kevin

■ RIGHT: An extra 1,000 seats are installed for Cherries' match against Aston Villa, October 1971

■ LEFT: Cherries ace goal-scorer Ted MacDougall poses with nine footballs to represent his triple hat-trick in the FA Cup against Margate

1971-1972 Record breaker Ted MacDougall scores nine of the eleven goals against Margate in the FA Cup first round tie November 1971

■ LEFT: Ted MacDougall receives his player of the month award for November from John Bond and Harold Walker in the Dean Court Supporters' Social Club

■ BELOW LEFT: John Sainty, John Benson, Fred Davies and Keith Miller take an 11am plunge with the Spartans

■ BELOW CENTRE: Harold Walker, chairman

RIGHT: A fan's unusual perch at Dean Court to watch his team draw 1-1 with Brighton

1971-1972

LEFT: Ted MacDougall scores two goals in Bournemouth's 3-1 win over Manchester United in a pre-season friendly at Dean Court

ABOVE: Cherries beat Grimsby 1-0, pictured Phil Boyer

RIGHT: Harry Redknapp watches the pre-season friendly against Tottenham, but injury prevents him from playing

BELOW: Team from August 1972

1972-1973

Redknapp joins Division Three Bournemouth in 1972 from West Ham United

LEFT: Cherries cup squad for the FA Cup game against Newcastle United

BOTTOM LEFT: Newcastle United v Bournemouth. Cherries are beaten by two goals in two minutes midway through the first half

BOTTOM CENTRE: Harry Redknapp in action

RIGHT: AFC Bournemouth v Oldham. Brian Clark leaps as Cherries slip into gear for the final push for promotion

BOTTOM RIGHT: Jimmy Gabriel against Halifax in April

Name changed to AFC Bournemouth in 1972, Bond and Walker wanted to give the club a more continental feel

1972-1973

■ LEFT: Tony Powell and Tommy Young in Cherries draw 1-1 at Tranmere

■ RIGHT: A jubilant John Parsons April 1974

■ BELOW LEFT: New Year's Day match at Dean Court against Brighton. The match ends 0-0

1973-1974

ABOVE CENTRE: Manager John Bond leaves Bournemouth for his new role at Norwich

- LEFT: Micky Cave 20th April 1974
- ABOVE: John Sainty
- RIGHT: John Deleaney, Micky Cave and Harry Wainman

BOTTOM CENTRE: Trevor Hartley becomes AFC Bournemouth manager in November 1974

■ RIGHT: AFC Bournemouth v Port Vale. Cherries lose 1-2 and plunge into the relegation zone, having already lost three home games in a row

■ BELOW CENTRE: Harry Redknapp July 1974

■ BELOW RIGHT: John Parsons, Howard Goddard and Steve Buttle. 19th October 1974

1974-1975

LEFT: John Wingate signs for AFC Bournemouth watched by Cherries' assistant manager Reg Tyrrell

■ ABOVE LEFT: Cherries start their FA Cup campaign with a 5-0 win against Southwick at Dean Court

■ ABOVE RIGHT: AFC Bournemouth v Charlton Athletic

■ ABOVE FAR RIGHT: Harry Redknapp and Charlie Williams with the Tunisia tournament winner's trophy 28th March 1975

■ ABOVE: AFC Bournemouth confirm appointment of former defender John Benson as player-manager. Benson pictured with Harold Walker

■ RIGHT: Cherries fans accompany the team to a tournament in Tunisia, which Bournemouth win by beating Millwall in the final

AFC Bournemouth travel to Tunisia to play in a tournament which they win by beating Millwall in the final

1974-1975

■ LEFT: AFC Bournemouth v Darlington. Cherries lost 1-2
■ BOTTOM: Police clear the stands and terraces to conduct a search after a bomb scare during the second half of Cherries' game against Southport. Nothing was found and the match was resumed and finished 3-3

1975-1976

LEFT: Keeper David Best returns to Cherries after a gap of nine years

■ ABOVE: Meet the new Cherries. Tom Paterson, Hughen Riley, Frank Barton and Peter Johnson August 1976

■ ABOVE RIGHT: AFC Bournemouth v Newport County

■ RIGHT: AFC Bournemouth shoot for the sun. Players have added incentive this season with the player of the year winning a holiday for two in Tenerife courtesy of John Plank Travel. A holiday in Majorca is also up for grabs for the first player to score 20 goals. John Plank is pictured donning the club strip and shooting for goal

AFC Bournemouth venture into the 1976-77 campaign in the Fourth Division with a pool of just 16 players

1976-1977

1977-1979

Cherries team photocall at the start of the 1977 season

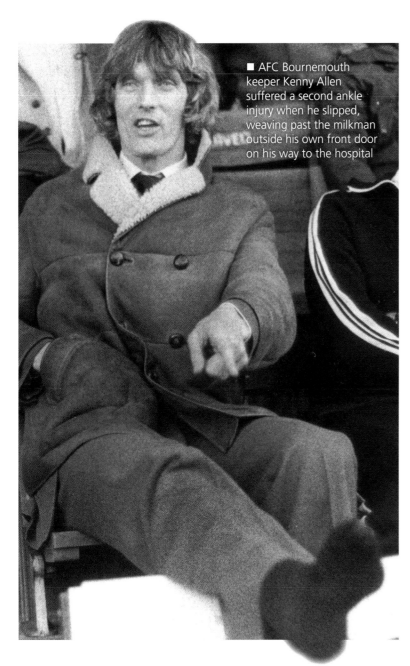

■ AFC Bournemouth keeper Kenny Allen suffered a second ankle injury when he slipped, weaving past the milkman outside his own front door on his way to the hospital

RIGHT: Ted MacDougall receives a silver salver in recognition of his 500th League appearance from AFCB vice-chairman Peter Hayward **1979-1980**

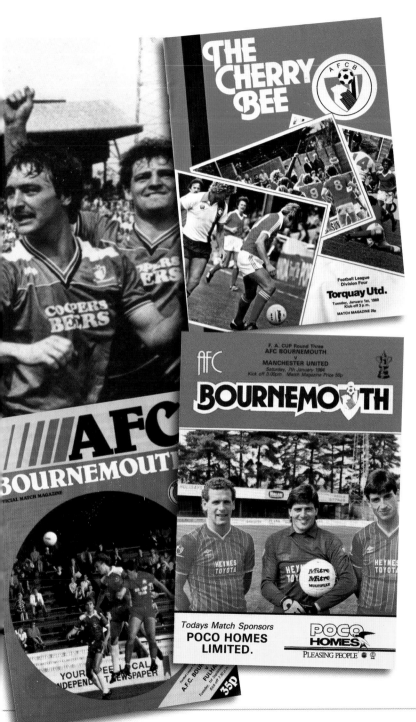

THE EIGHTIES

IT is hard to believe now that Harry Redknapp's first experience of managing the Cherries saw the club lose 9-0 to Lincoln and 5-0 to Leyton Orient.

That was in the season of 1982-83, when manager Dave Webb had been sacked after a string of poor results and Redknapp was filling in on a caretaker basis.

That season, Bournemouth had been in the headlines for signing George Best. But the once-great star played only five times, and the team ended that season in 14th place.

Redknapp became permanent manager after the 1983-84 season got off to a poor start and manager Don Megson quit.

The club began 1984 with the kind of giant-killing FA Cup tie that comes once in a generation – its 2-0 defeat of Manchester United in front of 15,000 at Dean Court. Bournemouth dominated the game and Redknapp called it "the greatest day of my football life".

But there was more success to come. While that season's League performance was less impressive, they were looking like promotion candidates the following year, and in 1987 the Cherries were finally going up after topping Division Three.

The club's fortunes fluctuated wildly in their first season in Division Two, and they started the 1988-89 season as relegation favourites.

Behind the scenes, a succession of take-overs and cash shortages did little to make the squad feel secure.

But, boosted by the inspired signing of prolific goal-scorer Luther Blissett from Watford, the Cherries clung on. And by the dawn of the 1990s, Redknapp was the club's longest-serving manager.

■ RIGHT: AFC Bournemouth team 1980-81

■ BELOW CENTRE: AFC team 1982: left to right, back row : Ian Leigh, Howard Goddard, Phil Brignull, Nigel Spackman, Tom Heffernan, Kenny Allen, Trevor Morgan, Paul Crompton, John Impey, Derek Dawkins, Harry Redknapp, coach, and David Webb, manager. Front row, Tony Funnell, Chris Sulley, Kevin Dawtry, Keith Williams, Steve Carter, Milton Graham and Brian O'Donnell. Wearing smart new tracksuits which they will take with them on a trip to New Zealand, by invitation from the New Zealand FA

■ FAR RIGHT: Kenny Allen May 1981

1980-1982

LEFT: Captain John Impey receives Mecca Loyalty Award for 200 league appearances from Jo Lucy, general manager of Tiffany's

■ BELOW LEFT: Harry Redknapp 9th October 1982

■ BELOW CENTRE: A delighted Trevor Morgan keeps his recent goal-a-game form against Chesterfield

■ BELOW LEFT: Harry Redknapp 9th October 1982

■ BOTTOM LEFT AND THIS PIC: 'Best hard pressed', George Best playing for AFC Bournemouth against Newport County in League Division 3 in March 1983

George Best made his Third Division debut for AFC Bournemouth against Newport County at Dean Court

1982-1983

■ BELOW: Manchester United fans arrive in Bournemouth ahead of their club's FA Cup match against AFC Bournemouth

■ BOTTOM LEFT: Cherries enjoy a meal at La Lupa 2 in Charminster the night before their FA Cup match against Man United

■ LEFT AND BELOW RIGHT: Ian Thompson and Milton Graham, goal scorers in AFC Bournemouth's FA Cup victory

1983-1984

AFC Bournemouth v Manchester United, FA Cup 3rd round, 7th January 1984

■ BELOW: AFC Bournemouth players Trevor Morgan, no 9, and Phil Brignull, background, celebrate the opening Cherries goal by Milton Graham as United centre-back Graeme Hogg looks on dejectedly

■ ABOVE: AFC Bournemouth celebrate their 2-0 victory

■ RIGHT: AFC Bournemouth squad and officials listening to the FA Cup draw following their win

■ BELOW: Players and officials visiting the mayor of Bournemouth, Cllr Jeanne Curtis, following their victory in the FA Cup over Manchester United

A fabulous 2-0 victory at Dean Court for AFC Bournemouth

1983-1984

■ Sean O'Driscoll attemps a shot, but Remi Moses is there to clear as AFC Bournemouth lose 3-0 at Old Trafford on 5th January 1985

■ TOP MIDDLE: Bournemouth's Billy Rafferty with Manchester United's Paul McGrath

■ ABOVE: It's all over as John Beck salutes the loyal Bournemouth fans at Old Trafford

■ LEFT: Bournemouth get a rousing send off from travelling fans after defeat in Manchester

1984-1985   For the second year running AFC Bournemouth draw Manchester United in the FA Cup 3rd round

■ RIGHT: Richard Cooke outfoxes Bury's veteran campaigner Mark Higgins at Dean Court, March 1987

■ BELOW CENTRE: Goalkeeper Gerry Peyton distributes the ball during the home game against Walsall, 11th April 1987

■ FAR RIGHT: John Williams. AFC Bournemouth v Darlington, 28th March 1987

BOTTOM LEFT: Demolition of the 'eyesore' Walker Stand at the Brighton Beach End of the ground, July 1985

1986-1987

1986-1987

AFC Bournemouth win the Division 3 title at Fulham on 4th May 1987

Cherries celebrate their league title win at the home game against Rotherham at Dean Court on 9th May 1987

1986-1987

- LEFT: Hands reach out for Harry at Bournemouth Town Hall
- RIGHT: Trevor Aylott in action at home to Bradford City 22nd August 1987
- BOTTOM LEFT: The team proudly toured from Dean Court to the Town Hall, on an open-top Yellow Coach
- BOTTOM RIGHT: Part of the delighted crowd at Bournemouth Town Hall

1986-1987

Fans cheer the Cherries all the way from their Dean Court ground to the civic reception at the Town Hall

■ RIGHT: Richard Cooke. AFC
Bournemouth v Bradford City 22nd
August 1987

■ RIGHT: David Armstrong controls
possession. AFC Bournemouth v
Bradford City 22nd August 1987

■ BELOW: Carl Richards AFC
Bournemouth v Barnsley

■ FAR RIGHT: Battle-scarred Tony
Pulis looks in determined mood

The Division 3 champions start the new season in Division 2

1987-1988

■ LEFT: Carl Richards AFC Bournemouth v Reading

■ BELOW CENTRE: Mark O'Connor beats Leicester City's Russell Osman. He almost gives Cherries a fourth minute lead, but Cherries lose 2-3

■ BELOW: Cherries' Mark O'Connor in pursuit of Southampton's Jimmy Case at Dean Court

1987-1988

Sean O'Driscoll, right, and Davy Puckett during the Southampton v Bournemouth game, 6th October 1987

Harry Redknapp receives his Third Division Manager of the Month award for October from Bell's regional executive Paul Stabb **1987-1988**

- ABOVE LEFT: Ian Bishop takes on Chelsea's Colin Pates
- BOTTOM LEFT: Richard Cooke after scoring against Chelsea
- LEFT: Cherries v Sunderland. Ian Bishop beats a challenge
- ABOVE RIGHT: Kevin Bond squares up to Hartlepool's Joe Allon in the FA Cup
- RIGHT: Cherries' fans queuing for FA Cup tickets against Manchester United

1988-1989

TOP CENTRE: Police horses on duty for the Chelsea game at Dean Court

■ BELOW: Fans queueing at Dean Court

■ BOTTOM: Veteran supporters Fred Bailey and Edwin Faulkner get their FA Cup tickets

■ TOP CENTRE: Aylott's magic moment as he scores the equaliser against United

■ BELOW CENTRE: Mark O'Connor tackles Gordon Strachan

■ LEFT: AFC Bournemouth v Manchester Utd

■ BELOW: Harry Redknapp calling the shots

■ BOTTOM RIGHT: Harry Redknapp with new signing Peter Shearer

AFC Bournemouth draw 1-1 with Manchester United in the FA Cup at Dean Court

1988-1989

■ BELOW: Cherries training

■ BOTTOM LEFT: Jamie Redknapp does a spot of painting at Dean Court

■ TOP CENTRE: Luther Blissett celebrates Cherries' 5th goal in their 5-4 victory over Hull City

■ LEFT: AFC Bournemouth v Oldham, 14th October 1989

■ BOTTOM MIDDLE: A pensive Harry Redknapp against Stoke City

1989-1990

ABOVE RIGHT: Cherries fans not impressed with 0-1 defeat against Sheffield United at Dean Court

■ BELOW: Kevin Bond against Portsmouth

■ BOTTOM: Bournemouth's Shaun Teale against Bradford City

ABOVE RIGHT: Leeds United fans riot at King's Park in May 1990

1989-1990

Official AFC Bournemouth Souvenir £2.50

WEMBLEY
A day to remember!

Produced in association
The Daily

AFC Bournemouth, the country's first Communit

We' you evermore

01425 277703

THE GREAT ESCAPE

The remarkable story of A.F.C. Bournemouth
1994/95

£3.00

AFC Bournemouth Centenary Celebration

1899 1999

AFC BOURNEMOUTH V LIVERPOOL FC

Wednesday 16th February 2000
Kick-off 7.45pm

OFFICIAL SOUVENIR PROGRAMME £2.50

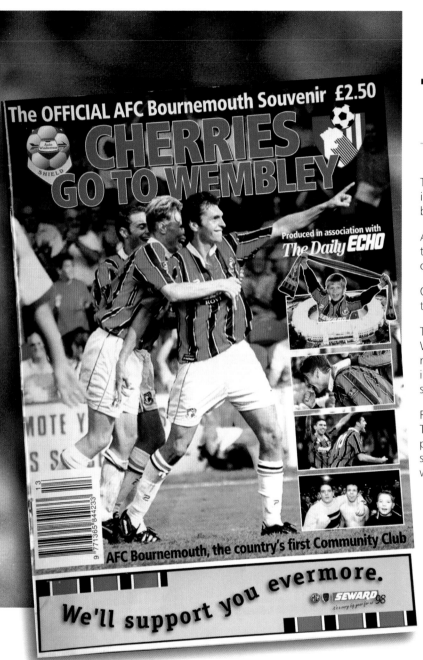

THE NINETIES

THE 1990s started with Bournemouth struggling to stay in the old Division Two – and everything came down to a bank holiday clash with Leeds United.

An estimated 6,000 Leeds fans came to Bournemouth that May weekend, many without tickets, and a hard core of them ran riot through the town.

On the pitch, Leeds' 1-0 victory ended Bournemouth's three years in the second division.

That summer, Harry Redknapp went to Italy for the World Cup with Brian Tiler, who had been the club's managing director. They were involved in road accident in which Tiler died, along with three young people in a sportscar that was on the wrong side of the road.

Redknapp left the club in 1992 and was succeeded by Tony Pulis. The club was suffering destabilising financial problems, the stadium was in poor repair and despite signings such as future legend Steve Fletcher, results were getting worse.

The 1994-95 season saw the Cherries struggling to avoid relegation from the new Division Two. Pulis was sacked, to be replaced by Mel Machin, and the team pulled off their 'Great Escape' from relegation.

But financial problems were worsening, and in 1997, the receivers were called in.

A meeting was held at the Winter Gardens concert hall, where £35,000 was donated in cash and a group of supporters announced a trust fund to buy the stadium.

The resulting stay of execution enabled the Cherries to make their first Wembley appearance in the final of the Auto Windscreens Shield in 1998.

They lost 2-1 to Grimsby after a "golden goal" in extra time; but being at Wembley at all seemed like a miracle.

ROCKETT
PLUMBING & HEATING SUPPLIES LTD

Book published in association with
www.rockettplumbing.co.uk

- LEFT: AFC Bournemouth pre-season training 23rd June 1990
- BOTTOM LEFT: Cherries players off to Army Camp. Young reserve keeper David McCarthy grabs probably his only opportunity ever to tell 6"1 Trevor Aylott, second left, what to do
- TOP RIGHT: Efan Ekoku, left, and Luther Blissett
- CENTRE: Paul Morrell, left, Harry Redknapp, centre, and Luther Blissett, right
- BOTTOM RIGHT: Trevor Aylott AFC Bournemouth v Fulham 29th September 1990. 3-0 League Division Three

1990-1991

LEFT: AFC Bournemouth players get called up to Army Camp

ABOVE: Sean O'Driscoll's 300th league game for AFC Bournemouth. Left to right Luther Blissett, Paul Morrell, Sean O'Driscoll and Andy Jones

BELOW: Andy Jones signing for AFC Bournemouth 25th Oct 1990

RIGHT: Jamie Redknapp in action for Bournemouth v Gillingham in the Leyland Daf Cup

BELOW: Short lived joy for Andy Jones and fans as the players mob Morrell. AFC lose the game 3-1 at Shrewsbury Town

BOTTOM RIGHT: Luther Blissett smashes in a penalty and jumps for joy as AFC Bournemouth beat Swansea City 1-0

1990-1991

■ BOTTOM LEFT: Fences come down at Dean Court 22nd June 1991

■ ABOVE CENTRE: Bournemouth fans at the Peterborough game at Dean Court

■ BOTTOM CENTRE: AFC Bournemouth v Newcastle United 5th January 1992

■ TOP RIGHT: Harry Redknapp urges his players on against Newcastle United

1991-1992

New signing Jimmy Case with AFC Bournemouth manager Harry Redknapp 3rd July 1991

■ LEFT: Denny Mundee scores Cherries' second goal as the Barnet keeper scrambles back in vain

■ BELOW: AFC Bournemouth 1992

RIGHT: Denny Mundee ends up in the net as Bournemouth beat Cheltenham 3-0

1992-1993

■ LEFT: Manager Tony Pulis aims to turn big striker Steve Fletcher from poodle to pitbull February 1993

■ BELOW: AFC Bournemouth football ground 5th March 1993

1992-1993

LEFT: Paul Morrell signs autographs at his testimonial match 4th May 1993

- RIGHT: Tony Pulis with his captain's choice Mark Morris
- TOP FAR RIGHT: Pitch invasion as AFC Bournemouth lose 1-2 to Wrexham at Dean Court 23rd April 1994
- BOTTOM CENTRE: Cherries lose 1-0 at Blackburn Rovers in the Coca-Cola League Cup 21st September 1993
- BELOW RIGHT: AFC Bournemouth fans want Pulis out 23rd April 1994

LEFT: Steve Cotterill celebrates his equaliser as AFC Bournemouth draw 1-1 with Bradford City 21st August 1993

1993-1994

■ LEFT: 16th August 1994, AFC Bournemouth v Northampton Town. Kevin Russell celebrates during the 2-0 Coca-Cola League Cup win

■ BELOW LEFT: 4th October 1994. AFC Bournemouth v Chelsea 0-1 Coca-Cola League Cup

■ TOP RIGHT: 27th December 1994, AFC Bournemouth v Crewe Alexandra, draw 1-1. Jason Brissett, left, and Crewe's Martyn Booty

■ CENTRE: 2nd May 1995, AFC Bournemouth v Shrewsbury Town, Mel Machin celebrates 3-0 win

Picture: Grahame Austin, Kitchenham Ltd

CENTRE: Aerial photo of Dean Court, 24th March 1995

LEFT: 2nd May 1995 AFC Bournemouth v Shrewsbury Town. The fans call for their heroes

RIGHT: AFC Bournemouth v Shrewsbury Town. Ian Andrews enjoys the 3-0 win

ABOVE LEFT AND RIGHT: Cherries players and fans celebrate staying up

1994-1995

■ TOP LEFT: 12th June 1995 Cherries pre-season training

■ TOP CENTRE: AFC Bournemouth team photo 1996

■ BOTTOM CENTRE: Steve Robinson celebrates his first goal, 30 November 1996 AFC Bournemouth v Luton Town

■ TOP AND BELOW RIGHT: Save the Cherries meeting at the Winter Gardens. Matt Holland centre stage. Fans give much needed cash

1995-1997

BOTTOM LEFT: Mel Machin and Harry Redknapp

■ BELOW: AFC Bournemouth v
Millwall 14 November 1996 - is this
the end for AFC Bournemouth?

RIGHT: Matt Holland with begging bowl asking people to donate money to save the club January 1997

1996-1997

■ TOP LEFT: Save the Cherries meeting at the Winter Gardens Bournemouth

■ TOP CENTRE: Back in action AFC Bournemouth trainer John Williams with Evening Echo sign 31st January 1997

■ BOTTOM RIGHT: Trust members and players celebrate launch of Europe's first community club

1997-1998

BOTTOM LEFT: Highlander barmaid Sarah Casey and team players raise their glasses to another fundraising bid

■ TOP LEFT: AFCB to Wembley. Tension turns to joy within a few moments

■ TOP MIDDLE: Ian Cox and John Bailey celebrate victory with the fans

■ RIGHT: Queues at Dean Court for Wembley tickets

■ BELOW: The squad for Wembley

BOTTOM LEFT: Fans celebrate their team going to Wembley

1997-1998

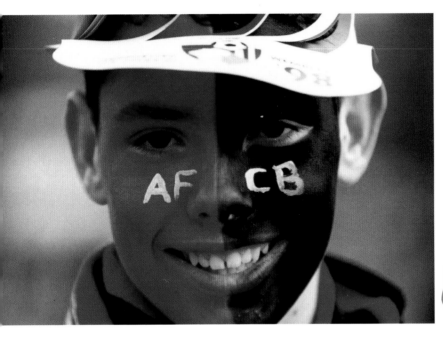

LEFT: Young fan Nigel Halligan at Wembley

BOTTOM LEFT: Suited and booted for Wembley left to right: Steve Robinson, John O'Neil, Eddie Howe, Russell Beardsmore, Jamie Vincent, Steve Fletcher, Mike Dean 15th April 1998

BELOW: John Bailey makes his entrance at Wembley

1997-1998

CENTRE: Players walk on to the pitch in the Auto Windscreens Shield at Wembley

■ LEFT AND BELOW LEFT: AFC Bournemouth fans at Wembley
■ TOP CENTRE: Steve Fletcher
■ MIDDLE CENTRE: Jason Brissett
■ BOTTOM CENTRE: Eddie Howe, Ian Cox, Jimmy Glass, Jamie Vincent and John O'Neill

BOTTOM RIGHT: John Bailey, Jamie Vincent and Neil Young applaud fans after their 2-1 defeat by Grimsby Town

1997-1998

■ LEFT: Eddie Howe with the Player of the Year trophy

■ BOTTOM LEFT: Chicago-bound tough guys Steve Robinson and Steve Fletcher

■ CENTRE TOP: Cherries' team picture 1998-99 season

■ BOTTOM CENTRE: Steve Robinson and Eddie Howe

■ RIGHT: Mohamed Berthe congratulates Mark Stein on his goal, to the delight of the Dean Court crowd, against Lincoln City

■ BELOW: Steve Fletcher against Wigan at Dean Court

1998-1999

ABOVE CENTRE: Steve Robinson, Northern Ireland, and Eddie Howe called up for England Under 21s

- TOP FAR LEFT: Players celebrate scoring against Basingstoke Town in the FA Cup first round
- CENTRE: One of Robinson's goals flies past the keeper against Wycombe at Dean Court
- TOP RIGHT: Steve Fletcher gets to grips with the Barnsley defence
- RIGHT MIDDLE: Steve Fletcher scores for AFC Bournemouth against Colchester at Dean Court 21st Aug 1999
- BOTTOM RIGHT: Second goal for Fletcher for AFC Bournemouth v Notts County in the FA Cup at Dean Court

ABOVE LEFT: FA Cup 3rd round, 2nd January 1999, Eddie Howe scores for AFC Bournemouth against West Brom at Dean Court

1999-2000

2000-2009

Sean O'Driscoll, who had served the club in various posts, was elevated to the position of manager at the start of the 2000-2001 season with Mel Machin taking on a director of football role.

O'Driscoll's first season at the helm will be remembered for a Division Two play-off near-miss, inspired by West Ham loan signing Jermain Defoe, who famously scored 10 goals in 10 games after starting the run on his debut at Stoke.

However, despite his goalscoring exploits, Cherries were pipped to a play-off place on the final day of the season following an epic 3-3 draw at Reading.

O'Driscoll was unable to save Cherries from relegation the following season but a maiden place in the play-offs was secured just 12 months later and the team bounced back at the first attempt.

A memorable May day at the Millennium Stadium in Cardiff saw Cherries overcome Lincoln 5-2 with club legend Steve Fletcher opening the scoring.

James Hayter scored a record-breaking hat-trick in 140 seconds against Wrexham the following season and, despite financial uncertainty, O'Driscoll managed to steady the ship until he left for Doncaster in October 2006.

O'Driscoll's successor Kevin Bond was unable to stave off relegation to the bottom flight in 2007-2008 while the club's future had been cast in doubt after it was placed into administration midway through the campaign.

Eddie Howe's appointment on New Year's Eve 2008 marked the dawn of an exciting and successful new era which started with a Houdini-like escape from relegation and continued with promotion to League One in 2009-2010.

Book published in association with
www.rockettplumbing.co.uk

Main picture by Michael Martin

■ LEFT: Steve Fletcher wins another header, at home to Nuneaton Borough in the FA Cup second round

■ BELOW: Wade Elliott tries to ride a Nuneaton challenge

2000-2001   Through to the third round: Richard Hughes and Wade Elliott celebrate the FA Cup win over Nuneaton

■ ABOVE: A new stadium and a new brand

■ RIGHT: Carl Fletcher in action against Bristol Rovers

■ RIGHT: November 2001 sees AFC Bournemouth beat Wrexham 3-0, in their first match at the new stadium

A new home: After a winning start, the season ends with the Cherries relegated to Division 3

2001-2002

■ LEFT: Fans hoping for autographs in their testimonial programmes

■ RIGHT: Mel acknowledges the support from the crowd

■ BOTTOM RIGHT: Mel and Rio Ferdinand who also had a spell at Dean Court, on loan

2002-2003

Thank you Mel: Manchester United come out with AFC Bournemouth for Mel Machin's testimonial match

The bigger they are... High fives after Carl Fletcher scores Cherries' second goal against United

2002-2003

■ LEFT: Scorer of two goals, Carl Fletcher celebrates in style

■ ABOVE: Steve Fletcher after hitting the net

■ BOTTOM LEFT: Fans' joy

■ BELOW: 'We're going up!' Players' celebrations on the pitch

■ RIGHT: Carl Fletcher is mobbed by team mates after scoring. The other scorers were Stephen Purches and Garreth O'Connor

2002-2003   PROMOTION: Millennium joy as Bournemouth thrash Lincoln City 5-2 in the Division 3 play-off final in Cardiff

TOP RIGHT: AFC Bournemouth celebrate promotion through the play-offs, and on the open-top bus parade

■ LEFT: Teddy Sheringham wins a header during the Bournemouth v Portsmouth testimonial match for Steve Fletcher

■ BELOW: Former AFCB player Richard Hughes in action for Portsmouth

■ TOP & RIGHT: Steve Fletcher acknowledges the support of team mates and crowd

2003-2004

Big appreciation for the Big Man

■ BELOW: Warren Cummings enjoys the moment after netting against Wycombe Wanderers

■ RIGHT: Stephen Purches celebrates the opener against Wrexham. James Hayter's hat-trick came after he came on as sub in the 84th minute. Bournemouth were leading 3-0, and Hayter made it 6-0 in 140 scintillating seconds, a Football League record

Record breaker: James Hayter, and newborn son, the day after scoring the fastest hat-trick in Football League history

2003-2004

■ TOP LEFT: Warren Cummings raids down the left against Wrexham

■ BOTTOM LEFT: Goalmouth action during Bournemouth v Chesterfield

■ LEFT: John Spicer celebrates a goal at Bradford, but the the linesman's flag rules it out

■ BELOW: Celebrations for Matthew Mills' equaliser at Bradford

■ BOTTOM CENTRE: Wade Elliott takes on the Bradford defence

2004-2005

Aerial superiority: Steve Fletcher rises unchallenged to power a header in his record-breaking appearance

TOP CENTRE: Andrew Surman is grabbed by team mates after scoring the winner against Gillingham

TOP RIGHT: James Coutts takes possession away from Rotherham United

BELOW: Bournemouth v Blackpool, Brett Pitman (right) celebrates his goal with Daryl Fordyce

BOTTOM RIGHT: It's there! Steve Fletcher is pursued by team mates after grabbing a goal at home to Brentford

2005-2006

■ TOP LEFT: Sean O'Driscoll waves goodbye to the Dean Court faithful, in his last match as Bournemouth manager, at home to Crewe Alexandra

■ LEFT: Kevin Bond after being named as the new Cherries manager

■ RIGHT: Darren Anderton acknowledges his first goal for Bournemouth at home to Leyton Orient

■ BOTTOM RIGHT: Steve Claridge runs out for Bournemouth v Port Vale, his 1000th competitive game

2006-2007

ABOVE: Sean's men, the AFC Bournemouth team photo 2006-07 season

■ BELOW: Jonathan Wilkes tackles Darren Anderton during the game

■ RIGHT: The AFC Bournemouth 2007-08 team photo

Famous faces: AFC Bournemouth v Luther Blissett XI, pro v celebrity match, the two teams together prior to kick-off

2007-2008

■ LEFT: Bournemouth v Leeds. Jem Karacan celebrates hitting the net for Bournemouth

■ RIGHT: Max Gradel enjoyed that

■ TOP RIGHT: Anguish on the touchline for Kevin Bond at home to Swansea

■ BOTTOM LEFT: Bournemouth v Millwall, Max Gradel pulls the trigger for Bournemouth's 2nd goal

■ TOP RIGHT: Anguish on the touchline for Kevin Bond at home to Swansea

■ BOTTOM RIGHT: Cherries' stalwart Neil Young announces his retirement, before the Bristol Rovers game, with Jeff Mostyn and Steve Sly

2007-2008 Cherries go into administration in February 2008, resulting in a 10 point deduction and relegation to League Division 2

REMARKABLE: Despite starting the season on minus 17 points, Eddie Howe galvanises the team and achieves The Greatest Escape **2008-2009**

- AFC Bournemouth manager Eddie Howe signs the Echo End The Ban petition
- TOP LEFT: Bournemouth v Grimsby, team mates celebrate Cherries' first goal with scorer Alan Connell
- BOTTOM LEFT: New chairman of AFC Bournemouth Eddie Mitchell, with Jason Tindall and Eddie Howe

2009-2010   CENTRE: Bournemouth v Rotherham United, manager Eddie Howe contemplates the situation on the touchline

■ BELOW: Steve Fletcher celebrates after heading in Bournemouth's first goal at home to Barnet

■ RIGHT: Alan Connell celebrates his goal against Burton with the fans

■ BOTTOM RIGHT: Eddie Howe faces the press after the Port Vale game

TOP AND BOTTOM LEFT: Promotion to League One. A remarkable achievement with a threadbare squad and a player embargo   **2009-2010**

■ LEFT: Jubilant fans

■ LEFT: All aboard! The AFC Bournemouth open-top bus victory parade along the seafront, celebrating promotion to League One

2009-2010

Eddie Mitchell and the board members amid the promotion celebrations

WE ARE GOING UP! WE ARE GOING UP! Fans' joy at the stadium and the seafront...

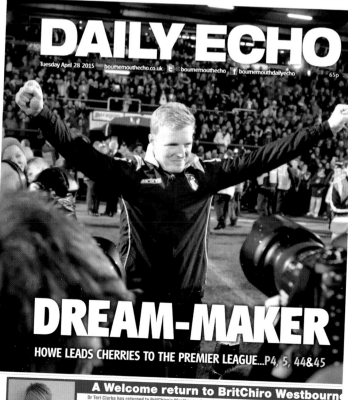

2010-2015

Following the club's rise back to League One under Eddie Howe, the young Cherries boss set his sights on a dramatic and unforeseen rise to the Championship.

He signed some key players: Winger Marc Pugh joined from Hereford and young midfielder Harry Arter from Woking. But Howe was forced to embark on his quest without Brett Pitman and Josh McQuoid, who left for Bristol City and Millwall, respectively.

The club's supporters then had to look on as Howe, himself, departed for Championship side Burnley in January 2011, with Lee Bradbury and Steve Fletcher taking the reins. Despite leading Cherries to the League One play-offs, Bradbury's men suffered semi-final penalty shoot-out heartache at Huddersfield Town.

Having watched most of that squad depart for pastures new, Bradbury was sacked with seven games of the 2011-12 season remaining, with Paul Groves appointed as the club's new manager permanently in the summer of 2012.

Groves soon found himself under pressure and was sacked after just one win in the opening 10 games of the 2012-13 season. With Cherries in 20th place in League One, Howe returned as manager to propel the club up the table, the season climaxing with promotion to the Championship.

A season of ups and downs saw Cherries finish 10th in English football's second flight, the club's highest ever finish, before some scintillating displays in the following campaign saw Howe's men win the Championship title and secure a first ever promotion to the Premier League.

Book published in association with
www.rockettplumbing.co.uk

135

■ LEFT: Danny Hollands celebrates a goal against Notts County at Dean Court

■ BELOW: Players and fans give applause for a minute's appreciation for the life of Keith Alexander, before the home game against Morecambe

2010-2011   Stand up for the big man: April 2010 sees Steve Fletcher applaud supporters in the new stand named in his honour

■ LEFT: AFC Bournemouth v
Hereford at Dean Court... Pitman's
goal celebration with Fletcher,
Hollands and Robinson

■ BELOW: Brett Pitman
wheels away in celebration
of a hat-trick for Cherries
at home to Peterborough

■ TOP RIGHT: Southampton v AFC
Bournemouth at St Mary's, Michael
Symes and Morgan Schneiderlin
battle for possession

BOTTOM RIGHT: Saints v Cherries, the players walk out onto the pitch at St Mary's Stadium

2010-2011

■ BELOW: December 2010, Bournemouth's groundsman James Lathwell surveys the snow covered pitch

■ RIGHT: January 2011, Chairman Eddie Mitchell and Bournemouth fans speak with one voice (or printer) about wanting Eddie Howe to stay at Dean Court

■ OPPOSITE: A pensive-looking Eddie on January 8, at his 99th and possibly final game managing Cherries, at home to Plymouth

■ FAR RIGHT TOP: They're staying! Eddie and Jason Tindall discuss their decision with the press outside the stadium in January 2011

■ FAR RIGHT BOTTOM: Just over two weeks later, Jan 28, Eddie Mitchell confirms the appointment of Lee Bradbury as manager with Steve Fletcher as player/assistant manager

2010-2011

A chill wind blows through Dean Court...

A fortnight is a long time in football...

2010-2011

■ RIGHT: Manager Lee Bradbury keeping a keen eye on proceedings in the Stevenage game

■ BELOW: Steve Fletcher receives an award to mark 600 league appearances for Bournemouth, before the game against Walsall

2011-2012

RIGHT: Wes Thomas in combative mood, competes for the ball against Bury at Dean Court

■ TOP LEFT: Manager Lee Bradbury in pensive mood

■ LEFT: Gillingham's keeper stretches in vain as Stephane Zubar, just seen behind Thomas, grabs the second goal for Cherries

■ BELOW: Back o' the net! Stephen Purches wheels away to celebrate scoring the opener against Gillingham

BOTTOM LEFT: The team and crowd observe a one minute silence for Remembrance Day before the game against Gillingham

2011-2012

- TOP LEFT: Teams and mascots walk out before the Tranmere fixture
- OUTSIDE CENTRE LEFT: Goal! Josh McQuoid is lovin' it, after scoring against Shrewsbury Town
- INSIDE CENTRE LEFT: Goal! Brett Pitman is congratulated after hitting the net against Crawley Town
- BOTTOM LEFT: Goal! Harry Arter celebrates scoring against Tranmere Rovers
- RIGHT: Eddie Howe giving an interview before the Leyton Orient game

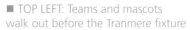

2012-2013

Catch me if you can... Marc Pugh shows serious intent as he tears down the touchline against Colchester

■ LEFT: Eddie Mitchell and Eddie Howe in buoyant mood after the game

■ RIGHT: Matt Ritchie gets them in a twist in the same game, Brett Pitman can't look...

■ BELOW: The players are on song

Let's celebrate: Promotion-winning Cherries get the bubbly out

2012-2013

WE ARE GOING UP!

2012-2013

The Cherries' open top bus tour passes through a crowd-lined Bournemouth town centre

Bournemouth

- TOP LEFT: Howe, Tindall and Ancelotti
- LEFT: Shaun MacDonald battles Ronaldo
- BELOW LEFT: Ronaldo, Benzema et al greet the Cherries players and mascots
- RIGHT: Ted MacDougall opens the new stand named in his honour

2013-2014

The Real Deal: Madrid bring a Galactico-filled side to Dean Court for a pre-season friendly!

Cameras at the ready, as Ronaldo takes a free kick and Harry Arter takes on Benzema in the air

2013-2014

- **LEFT:** Stephen Purches walks out, with his children, between the teams before his testimonial game against West Ham United
- **BELOW LEFT:** Brett Pitman and Lewis Grabban battle for the ball
- **BELOW:** Wes Thomas wins an aerial duel
- **RIGHT:** Steven Gerrard leads out the Liverpool team before their cup tie at Bournemouth
- **BELOW RIGHT:** Eddie Howe greets Brendan Rodgers
- **BOTTOM RIGHT:** Andrew Surman gets tight to Luis Suarez

2013-2014   Cherries take on West Ham, in Stephen Purches' testimonial game, and Liverpool in the FA Cup 4th round

■ LEFT: Marc Pugh runs away from Gerrard with the ball

■ BELOW: Harry Arter shows determination in a challenge with Gerrard

RIGHT: 'I played the ball ref', Arter and Ritchie protest innocence but Luis Suarez isn't convinced

2013-2014

■ BELOW: Andrew Surman's celebrations after his goal at home to Leeds United

■ TOP CENTRE: Eunan O'Kane scores against West Bromwich Albion

■ BOTTOM CENTRE: Simon Francis celebrates Callum Wilson's goal against Charlton Athletic

■ TOP RIGHT: Bournemouth v Millwall, Brett Pitman celebrates netting Bournemouth's second goal

■ BOTTOM RIGHT: Callum Wilson slides the ball past West Brom's goalkeeper and into the net

2014-2015

Hat-trick hero: Marc Pugh with match ball at Birmingham

It's been emotional...

- ABOVE: Bournemouth v Cardiff, Steve Cook celebrates with Harry Arter after his goal
- BELOW: That amazing scoreline
- RIGHT: Brett Pitman rises to beat the Cardiff defence
- TOP CENTRE: Three Fulham defenders can't stop Brett Pitman nodding it into their net
- BOTTOM CENTRE: Harry Arter scores away at Millwall
- TOP RIGHT: Cherry Bear flies the flag
- BOTTOM RIGHT: Matt Ritchie celebrates a goal at home to Sheffield Wednesday

90+5

CHERRIES 5
CARDIFF 3

2014-2015

2014-2015

■ Dean Court in rapture.
The unbelievable has come true!
AFC Bournemouth have won
promotion to the Premier League.
Fans, players, manager and
chairman celebrate as one...

'We are Premier League! We are Premier League!'

2014-2015

2014-2015 Saturday 2nd May. Even better: Eddie and the fans enjoy the moment at Charlton Athletic, where the Championship is won

The Sky Bet Champions 2015: AFC Bournemouth!

2014-2015

FAN-TASTIC! The town celebrates with the Cherries by the sea on the open-top bus parade

August 22nd 2015, Callum Wilson's hat-trick sinks West Ham at the Boleyn Ground for Cherries' first Premier League victory... **2015-2016**

WHO DID WHAT

Pictures taken by past and present Daily Echo staff and freelance photographers including ;

Bruce Adams, Sally Adams, Harry Ashley, Stan Banks, Jon Beal, John Beasley, Andy Burbidge, Richard Crease, Paul Collins, Mick Cunningham, John Gilbride, Jo Harvell, Andy Horsfield, Duncan Lee, Red Leyden, Martin Lodge, Corin Messer, Hattie Miles, Tom Morris, Denis Murphy, Andy Scaysbrook, Sam Sheldon, P.Smith, Jim Sowerby, Pat Timmons

Picture research and sourcing: Michelle Luther, Michaela Horsfield

Design and page layout: David Hewitt, John Nesbitt

Words: Darren Slade, Neil Perrett, Neil Meldrum

Book sales: Marie Rushall

Editor: Andy Martin

Published by:

DAILY ECHO

bournemouthecho.co.uk

PICTURE THIS

Echo pictures within this book are available to purchase in a range of print sizes.

If you would like to order one or more prints please:

- Call into a Daily Echo office and fill in an order form
- Visit bournemouthecho.co.uk and click on 'photos'
- For further information call us on 01202 411425
- Book sales: 01202 292250

Published by: Newsquest Media (Southern) Ltd, Richmond Hill, Bournemouth BH2 6HH

© Newsquest Media (Southern) Ltd

First published in 2015

ISBN 978-0-9933533-1-4

A selection of the photographs in this book can be viewed at: bournemouthecho.co.uk/afcbbook